D0587419

Heavenly Cupcakes

by Nancy Lambert

Licensed exclusively to Top That Publishing Ltd
Tide Mill Way, Woodbridge, Suffolk, IP12 1AP, UK
www.topthatpublishing.com
Copyright © 2014 Tide Mill Media.
All rights reserved
0 2 4 6 8 9 7 5 3 1
Printed and bound in China

CONTENTS

INTRODUCTION

e term 'cupcake' was first used in an 1828 cookbook and got its name from
individual pottery cups they were baked in. Since then, the fancy little
es have enjoyed much-deserved success and have grown even more
oular in recent years. From the mouth-watering icing to the fluffy base, a
tastically made cupcake is guaranteed to appeal and bring a smile to
one's face!

s book will provide you with a selection of cupcake recipes that are perfect
junior chefs to make with the help of an adult. And remember, once you
e perfected the recipes, don't be afraid to experiment with the ingredients
d toppings to create your own great cupcake treats!

COOKING TIPS!

Make sure you use the freshest ingredients possible.

All of the cupcakes in this book feature butter, but margarine works just
s well.

ill your paper cases so they are about two-thirds full. Don't fill them too
igh or they will spill over whilst in the oven.

Cupcakes are best eaten the day they are made, however plain cupcakes
an be frozen for up to three months.

Cupcakes are cooked once a toothpick pricked into the middle of the cake
omes out clean.

EQUIPMENT

- To complete the recipes in this book, you will need to use a selection of every cooking equipment and utensils, such as mixing bowls, saucepans, a sieve, knives spoons and forks and a chopping board.

- Of course, you'll need to weigh and measure the ingredients, so you'll need a measuring jug and some kitchen scales too.

- Some of the recipes tell you to use a whisk. Ask an adult to help you use an electric whisk, or you can use a balloon whisk yourself — you'll just have to wor extra hard!

- All of the recipes in this book need bun cases and a bun case baking tray. Befor starting any recipe, put the cases into the tray and preheat the oven. All other equipment that you may not have to hand are listed at the start of each recipe

SAFETY & HYGIENE

**ADULT SUPERVISION
IS REQUIRED FOR
ALL RECIPES**

- Before starting any cooking always wash your hands.

- Cover any cuts with a plaster.

- Wear an apron to protect your clothes.

- Always make sure that all the equipment you use is clean.

- If you need to use a sharp knife to cut up something hard, ask an adult to help you. Always use a chopping board.

- Remember that trays in the oven and pans on the cooker can get very hot. Always ask an adult to turn on the oven and to get things in and out of the ove for you.

- Always ask an adult for help if you are using anything electrical — like an electric whisk.

- Be careful when heating anything in a pan on top of the cooker. Keep the hand turned to one side to avoid accidentally knocking the pan.

- Keep your pets out of the kitchen while cooking.

GETTING STARTED

MEASURING

Use scales to weigh exactly how much of each ingredient you need or use a measuring jug to measure liquids.

MIXING

Use a spoon, balloon whisk or electric hand whisk to mix the ingredients together.

DIFFERENT IDEAS

Decorate your cupcakes with flavoured or coloured icing, and then add chocolate drops, sweets or sugar strands.

CREATING RECIPES

Once you've made a recipe in this book a few times, think about whether you could make your own version. This way you can start to make up your own recipes. Try to think up names for the things you create!

PLEASE NOTE

The measurements given in this book are approximate. Use the same measurement conversions throughout your recipe (grams or ounces) to maintain the correct ratios. All of the recipes in this book have been created for adults to make with junior chefs and must not be attempted by an unsupervised child.

Read through each recipe to make sure you've got all the ingredients that you need before you start.

PLAIN CUPCAKES

Ingredients:
- 125 g (4 ¹/₂ oz) self-raising flour
- 125 g (4 ¹/₂ oz) butter, softened
- 125 g (4 ¹/₂ oz) caster sugar
- 2 large eggs
- 2–3 tablespoons milk

1 Preheat the oven to 180°C / 350°F / gas mark 4.

2 Sift the flour into a bowl, followed by the butter. Use the tips of your fingers to rub the butter and flour together until the mixture becomes crumbly. Alternatively, ask an adult to use an electric whisk.

3 Add the sugar and mix it in, then stir in the eggs. Finally, add the milk to make the mixture creamy.

4 Put spoonfuls of the mixture into the bun cases. Bake the cupcakes for 10–15 minutes, until they are golden brown, then leave them to cool on a wire rack.

TOP TIP!
Make sure the oven is the required temperature before you place the cupcakes inside!

ALENTINE CUPCAKES

equipment:

te of paper cut into a

art shape

dients:

) g (4 oz) self-raising flour

ablespoon cocoa powder

5 g (4 1/2 oz) butter,

gened

5 g (4 1/2 oz) caster sugar

arge eggs

3 tablespoons milk

he topping:

g sugar

1 Preheat the oven to 180°C / 350°F / gas mark 4.

2 Sift the flour and cocoa powder into a bowl.

3 Put the butter in the bowl. Use the tips of your fingers to rub the butter, flour and cocoa powder together until the mixture becomes crumbly. Alternatively, ask an adult to use an electric whisk.

4 Add the sugar and mix it in, then stir in the eggs.

5 Finally, add the milk to make the mixture creamy.

6 Put spoonfuls of the mixture into the bun cases. Bake the cupcakes for 10–15 minutes, then leave them to cool on a wire rack.

7 Leave the cupcakes until they are cool, then hold the heart-shaped paper cut-out over the top of the cake whilst you sprinkle over the icing sugar.

TOP TIP!
Experiment with different shaped cut-outs, such as stars, moons and swirls.

CUPCAKE NESTS

Extra equipment:
- piping bag

Ingredients:
- 250 g (9 oz) plain flour, sifted
- 100 g (4 oz) sugar
- 1/2 teaspoon baking powder
- 1 teaspoon bicarbonate of soda
- 100 g (4 oz) butter
- 100 g (4 oz) dark chocolate
- 180 ml (6 fl.oz) water
- 2 eggs
- 180 ml (6 fl.oz) milk
- a few drops of vanilla essence

For the topping:
- 150 g (5 oz) butter, softened
- 250 g (9 oz) icing sugar
- 2 tablespoons cocoa powder
- chocolate eggs

1 Preheat the oven to 180°C / 350°F / gas mark 4.

2 Put the sifted flour, sugar, baking powder, bicarbonate of soda and butter in a large bowl. Mix together.

3 Next, ask an adult to melt the dark chocolate in a heatproof bowl over a pan of hot water. Make sure the water doesn't touch the bottom of the bowl.

4 Add the water, eggs, milk, vanilla essence and melted chocolate to the flour mixture.

5 Beat together until thoroughly mixed.

6 Use a teaspoon to transfer equal amounts of the mixture to the bun cases. Bake the cupcakes for 20–25 minutes. Leave them to cool on a rack.

7 For the topping, beat together the butter and icing sugar. Combine the cocoa powder with a little water, and add to the mixture. Beat until smooth and creamy.

8 Place the topping into a piping bag and pipe onto each cupcake. Top with a chocolate egg.

TOP TIP!
Purchase some decorative edible flowers for a nice seasonal display.

ANOFFEE CUPCAKES

equipment:

g bag

ents:

g (4 oz) butter, softened

g (2 oz) caster sugar

g (2 oz) dulce de leche

gs, lightly beaten

nall ripe bananas

g (4 1/2 oz) self-raising

r, sifted

tsp baking powder

e topping:

pped cream

toffee, broken into pieces,

ecorate

1 Preheat the oven to 180°C / 350°F / gas mark 4.

2 Place the butter in a bowl, then beat in the sugar and the dulce de leche until smooth and creamy.

3 Beat in the eggs, a quarter at a time, making sure each lot is well mixed in before adding the next.

4 Peel and thoroughly mash the bananas before adding to the mixture. Stir in well.

5 Finally, fold in the sifted flour and baking powder and beat for a couple of seconds to combine.

6 Put spoonfuls of the mixture into the bun cases. Bake the cupcakes for 10–15 minutes, then leave them to cool on a wire rack.

7 Once cool, place the whipped cream into a piping bag and pipe onto the top of the cupcakes.

8 Finish off with a sprinkling of broken toffee pieces.

TOP TIP!
Don't worry if your bananas are slightly too ripe or bruised – the recipe works just as well.

HALLOWEEN CUPCAKES

TOP TIP! Try out different spooky decorations – skeletons, witches' hats or bats!

Extra equipment:
- icing syringe

Ingredients:
- 125 g (4 1/2 oz) self-raising flour
- 125 g (4 1/2 oz) butter, softened
- 125 g (4 1/2 oz) caster sugar
- 2 eggs
- a few drops of vanilla extract
- 2–3 tablespoons milk

For the topping:
- 140 g (5 oz) butter, softened
- 280 g (10 oz) icing sugar
- 1–2 tablespoons milk
- a few drops of orange food colouring

For the spider:
- 1 egg white
- 100 g (4 oz) icing sugar
- a few drops of black food colouring

1 Preheat the oven to 180°C / 350°F / gas mark 4.

2 Sift the flour into a bowl, followed by the butter. Use the tips of your fingers to rub the butter and flour together until the mixture becomes crumbly. Alternatively, ask an adult to use an electric whisk. Add the sugar and mix it in, then stir in the eggs. Finally, add the vanilla extract and milk to make the mixture creamy.

3 Put spoonfuls of the mixture into the bun cases. Bake the cupcakes for 10–15 minutes, until they are golden brown, then leave them to cool on a wire rack.

4 For the topping, place the butter in a large bowl and add half the icing sugar.

5 Beat until smooth. Add the remaining icing sugar and one tablespoon of the milk and beat the mixture until creamy and smooth. Beat more milk if necessary to loosen the icing. Stir in the orange food colouring until well combined, then spread the topping onto the top of each cupcake.

6 To make the spider: beat an egg white in a bowl. Sift the icing sugar into the bowl. Beat the mixture until the icing becomes smooth and thick. Add a few drops of black food colouring, then spoon the icing into an icing syringe. Carefully pipe your spider decoration onto the cupcakes. Ask an adult to run a knife carefully along the spider to add texture.

ARSHMALLOW CUPCAKES

equipment:

ng bag

ients:

g (4 1/2 oz) self-raising

g (4 1/2 oz) butter,
ened

g (4 1/2 oz) caster sugar

rge eggs

tablespoons milk

large pink marshmallows

e topping:

g (7 oz) pink marshmallows

g (1 lb) butter, softened

g (1 lb) icing sugar

ew drops of vanilla essence

i marshmallows, to decorate

ar sprinkles

1 Preheat the oven to 180°C / 350°F / gas mark 4.

2 Sift the flour into a bowl, followed by the butter. Use the tips of your fingers to rub the butter and flour together until the mixture becomes crumbly. Alternatively, ask an adult to use an electric whisk.

3 Add the sugar and mix it in, then stir in the eggs. Finally, add the milk to make the mixture creamy.

4 Put spoonfuls of the mixture into the bun cases, half filling each case. Place a marshmallow into the middle, then top with the remaining mixture. Bake the cupcakes for 15–20 minutes, until they are golden brown, then leave them to cool on a wire rack.

5 For the topping, add the pink marshmallows and butter to a pan and ask an adult to heat for a couple of minutes, then leave to cool.

6 Next, sift the icing sugar into the mixture and add the vanilla essence. Stir well to combine.

7 Place the mixture into a piping bag and pipe onto each of the cupcakes. Top with mini marshmallows and sugar sprinkles to finish.

TOP TIP!
If you have any marshmallows left over, place them on top of a hot chocolate with a big dollop of whipped cream – yummy!

CREAMY CHOCOLATE CUPCAKES

Extra equipment:
• piping bag

Ingredients:
• 100 g (4 oz) self-raising flour
• 1 tablespoon cocoa powder
• 125 g (4 ½ oz) butter, softened
• 125 g (4 ½ oz) caster sugar
• 2 large eggs
• 2–3 tablespoons milk

For the topping:
• whipped cream
• a few drops of vanilla essence

1 Preheat the oven to 180°C / 350°F / gas mark 4.

2 Sift the flour and cocoa powder into a bowl.

3 Put the butter in the bowl. Use the tips of your fingers to rub the butter, flour and cocoa powder together until the mixture becomes crumbly. Alternatively, ask an adult to use an electric whisk.

4 Add the sugar and mix it in, then stir in the eggs.

5 Finally, add the milk to make the mixture creamy.

6 Put spoonfuls of the mixture into the bun cases. Bake the cupcakes for 10–15 minutes, then leave them to cool on a wire rack.

7 Once cool, place the whipped cream, mixed with the vanilla essence, into a piping bag and pipe onto the top of the cupcakes.

TOP TIP!
Try using different flavoured essences in the creamy topping.

14

HOC-CHIP COOKIE CUPCAKES

equipment:

ing pin

i cookie cutters

ing bag

ients:

Plain Cupcakes, page 6

e cookies:

g (12 oz) plain flour

easpoon bicarbonate of soda

g (8 oz) butter

g (6 ½ oz) caster sugar

g (6 ½ oz) soft brown sugar

few drops of vanilla extract

eggs

g (4 oz) chocolate chips

topping:

g (5 oz) butter, softened

g (10 oz) icing sugar

2 tablespoons milk

ocolate chips, to decorate

1 Preheat the oven to 180°C / 350°F / gas mark 4.

2 Follow the plain cupcake recipe on page 6, but also add chocolate chips to the mixture before placing the mixture into the bun cases.

3 Whilst the cupcakes are cooking, make the cookies. First, combine the flour and bicarbonate of soda in a bowl.

4 In another bowl, combine the butter, sugar, brown sugar and vanilla extract until creamy. Beat in the eggs.

5 Gradually beat in the flour mixture and stir in the chocolate chips.

6 Then, roll the mixture out and use a cookie cutter to cut out mini cookie shapes. Lay on a baking tray, spaced widely apart and bake for 9–11 minutes.

7 For the topping, place the butter in a large bowl and add half of the icing sugar. Beat until smooth. Add the remaining icing sugar and one tablespoon of the milk and beat the mixture until creamy and smooth. Beat in more milk if necessary to loosen the icing.

8 Add the topping to a piping bag and pipe onto the top of each cooled cupcake. Top with a sprinkle of chocolate chips and a mini cookie.

TOP TIP!
Serve with a cup of hot chocolate!

15

PRETTY IN PINK CUPCAKES

Ingredients:
- 125 g (4 ¹/₂ oz) self-raising flour
- 125 g (4 ¹/₂ oz) butter, softened
- 125 g (4 ¹/₂ oz) caster sugar
- 2 large eggs
- 2–3 tablespoons milk

For the topping:
- 140 g (5 oz) butter, softened
- 280 g (10 oz) icing sugar
- 1–2 tablespoons milk
- a few drops of pink food colouring
- sugar sprinkles

1 Preheat the oven to 180°C / 350°F / gas mark 4.

2 Sift the flour into a bowl, followed by the butter. Use the tips of your fingers to rub the butter and flour together until the mixture becomes crumbly. Alternatively, ask an adult to use an electric whisk.

3 Add the sugar and mix it in, then stir in the eggs.

4 Finally, add the milk to make the mixture creamy.

5 Put spoonfuls of the mixture into the bun cases. Bake the cupcakes for 10–15 minutes, until they are golden brown, then leave them to cool on a wire rack.

6 For the topping, place the butter in a large bowl and add half of the icing sugar. Beat until smooth. Add the remaining icing sugar and one tablespoon of the milk and beat the mixture until creamy and smooth. Beat in more milk if necessary to loosen the icing.

7 Stir in the pink food colouring until well combined, then swirl onto the top of each cupcake. Top with sugar sprinkles to finish.

TOP TIP! These cupcakes will go down brilliantly at a party. For added 'wow' factor, display them with a pink feather boa backdrop!

PIRATE CUPCAKES

equipment:

g syringe

ients:

g (4 ½ oz) self-raising
r

g (4 ½ oz) butter,
ened

g (4 ½ oz) caster sugar

arge eggs

tablespoons milk

e topping:

gg white

g (4 oz) icing sugar

d colouring

ets, to decorate

1 Preheat the oven to 180°C / 350°F / gas mark 4.

2 Sift the flour into a bowl, followed by the butter. Use the tips of your fingers to rub the butter and flour together until the mixture becomes crumbly. Alternatively, ask an adult to use an electric whisk.

3 Add the sugar and mix it in, then stir in the eggs. Finally, add the milk to make the mixture creamy.

4 Put spoonfuls of the mixture into the bun cases. Bake the cupcakes for 10–15 minutes, until they are golden brown, then leave them to cool on a wire rack.

5 To make the topping, beat the egg white in a small bowl. Sift the icing sugar into the bowl and beat the mixture until the icing becomes smooth and thick.

6 Spoon two thirds of the icing onto each cupcake, smoothing down with a knife or spatula. Leave the icing to set and then repeat the process, this time adding food colouring to the remaining icing and using an icing syringe to add the finer pirate details.

7 Top with sweets to finish.

TOP TIP! Why not give each of your pirates a different face?

CHRISTMAS CUPCAKES

Extra equipment:
- rolling pin
- cookie cutters, various shapes

Ingredients:
- 100 g (4 oz) self-raising flour
- 1 tablespoon cocoa powder
- 125 g (4 ½ oz) butter, softened
- 125 g (4 ½ oz) caster sugar
- 2 large eggs
- 2–3 tablespoons milk

For the topping:
- ready-to-roll icing
- red food colouring
- green food colouring
- sweets or silver balls

1 Preheat the oven to 180°C / 350°F / gas mark 4.

2 Sift the flour and cocoa powder into a bowl, followed by the butter. Use the tips of your fingers to rub the butter, flour and cocoa powder together until the mixture becomes crumbly.

3 Add the sugar and mix it in, then stir in the eggs.

4 Finally, add the milk to make the mixture creamy.

5 Put spoonfuls of the mixture into the bun cases. Bake the cupcakes for 10–15 minutes, then leave them to cool on a wire rack.

6 For the topping, roll out some of the ready-to-roll icing and cut out shape with cookie cutters. Lay over a few of the cupcakes.

7 Next, knead a couple of drops of re food colouring into some of the remaining icing. When the colour is even, roll out the icing and cut out festive shape Repeat the process, this time with the gre food colouring.

8 Lay the different shapes over the tops of the rest of the cupcakes and finish with sweets or silver balls.

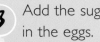
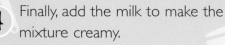

TOP TIP!
Pipe extra decorations onto the top of the cupcakes with royal icing, using a piping bag with a thin nozzle.

INI CUPCAKES

equipment:

ni bun case baking tray

ni bun cases

ing bag

dients:

5 g (4 ½ oz) self-raising
ur

5 g (4 ½ oz) butter,
tened

5 g (4 ½ oz) caster sugar

large eggs

-3 tablespoons milk

the topping:

0 g (5 oz) butter, softened

0 g (10 oz) icing sugar

-2 tablespoons milk

ible flowers, to decorate

1 Preheat the oven to 180°C / 350°F / gas mark 4.

2 Sift the flour into a bowl, followed by the butter. Use the tips of your fingers to rub the butter and flour together until the mixture becomes crumbly. Alternatively, ask an adult to use an electric whisk.

3 Add the sugar and mix it in, then stir in the eggs.

4 Finally, add the milk to make the mixture creamy.

5 Put spoonfuls of the mixture into the mini bun cases. Bake the cupcakes for 8–10 minutes, until they are golden brown, then leave them to cool on a wire rack.

6 For the topping, place the butter in a large bowl and add half of the icing sugar. Beat until smooth. Add the remaining icing sugar and one tablespoon of the milk and beat the mixture until creamy and smooth. Beat in more milk if necessary to loosen the icing.

7 Place the topping into a piping bag and pipe over each of the mini cupcakes.

8 Finish with an edible flower and serve.

TOP TIP! Always allow your cupcakes to completely cool before decorating.

COLOURFUL CUPCAKES

Extra equipment:
• rolling pin
• cookie cutters

Ingredients:
• 225 g (8 oz) self-raising flour
• 80 g (3 oz) butter
• 80 g (3 oz) caster sugar
• 1 egg
• 75–100 ml (3–4 fl.oz) milk

For the topping:
• ready-to-roll icing
• food colouring

1 Preheat the oven to 180°C / 350°F / gas mark 4.

2 Sift the flour into a bowl, followed by the butter. Use your fingertips to rub the butter and flour together until the mixture becomes crumbly.

3 Add the sugar and mix it in, then stir in the egg. Finally, add enough milk to make the mixture creamy.

4 Put spoonfuls of the mixture into the bun cases. Bake the buns for 10–15 minutes, until they are golden brown, then leave them to cool.

5 For the decorative topping, knead a couple of drops of food colouring into some of the icing. When the colour is even, roll out the icing and cut out shapes, either with a cookie cutter or ask an adult to use a sharp knife. Lay the different shapes over the tops of the cupcakes.

6 Repeat the process, with different food colourings and icing shapes.

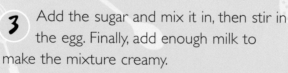

TOP TIP!
Experiment with different shapes and colours. Try to make each cupcake look different!

22

MAKES 12

equipment:
dles

ients:
g (4 oz) self-raising flour
ablespoon cocoa powder
g (4 1/2 oz) butter,
ened
g (4 1/2 oz) caster sugar
arge eggs
3 tablespoons milk

he topping:
ew drops of vanilla essence
) g (4 oz) whipped cream
gar sprinkles
dles, to decorate

1 Preheat the oven to 180°C / 350°F / gas mark 4.

2 Sift the flour and cocoa powder into a bowl.

3 Put the butter in the bowl. Use the tips of your fingers to rub the butter, flour and cocoa powder together until the mixture becomes crumbly. Alternatively, ask an adult to use an electric whisk.

4 Add the sugar and mix it in, then stir in the eggs.

5 Finally, add the milk to make the mixture creamy.

6 Put spoonfuls of the mixture into the bun cases. Bake the cupcakes for 10–15 minutes, then leave them to cool on a wire rack.

7 For the topping, add the vanilla essence to the whipped cream. Place in a piping bag, then swirl over each of the cupcakes.

8 Top each with sugar sprinkles and girlie candles.

TOP TIP!
Set a timer so you don't forget about your cupcakes cooking in the oven!

JELLY BEAN JAM CUPCAKES

Ingredients:
- 125 g (4 ½ oz) self-raising flour
- 125 g (4 ½ oz) butter, softened
- 125 g (4 ½ oz) caster sugar
- 2 large eggs
- 2–3 tablespoons milk
- 100 g (4 oz) fruit jam

For the topping:
- 100 g (4 oz) icing sugar
- 1–2 tablespoons hot water
- a few drops of pink food colouring
- 12 jelly beans

1 Preheat the oven to 180°C / 350°F / gas mark 4.

2 Sift the flour into a bowl, followed by the butter. Use the tips of your fingers to rub the butter and flour together until the mixture becomes crumbly. Alternatively, ask an adult to use an electric whisk.

3 Add the sugar and mix it in, then stir in the eggs.

4 Finally, add the milk to make the mixture creamy.

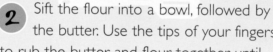

5 Put spoonfuls of the mixture into the bun cases, filling them halfway. Drop a teaspoonful of jam on top of the mixture and then cover with the remaining mixture.

6 Bake the cupcakes for 10–15 minutes, until they are golden brown, then leave them to cool on a wire rack.

7 To make the topping, sift the icing sugar into a bowl and add 1–2 tablespoons of hot water. Mix until you have a thick paste.

8 Add one or two drops of pink food colouring. Once well mixed, spoon the icing onto each cupcake and top with a jelly bean.

TOP TIP!
Add more than one jelly bean to each cupcake if you like!

AVENDER CUPCAKES

equipment:

der

ents:

teaspoon dried lavender

ers

g (4 ¹/₂ oz) caster sugar

g (4 ¹/₂ oz) butter,

ened

rge eggs

g (4 ¹/₂ oz) self-raising

tablespoons milk

e topping:

g (5 oz) butter, softened

g (10 oz) icing sugar

tablespoons milk

ets, to decorate

1 Preheat the oven to 180°C / 350°F / gas mark 4.

2 Place the lavender flowers into a blender and ask an adult to process.

3 Add the flowers to a bowl, followed by the sugar and butter. Mix well to combine and then beat in the eggs.

4 Sift in the flour and fold to combine. Finally, add the milk to make the mixture creamy.

5 Put spoonfuls of the mixture into the bun cases. Bake the cupcakes for 10–15 minutes, until they are golden brown, then leave them to cool on a wire rack.

6 For the topping, place the butter in a large bowl and add half of the icing sugar. Beat until smooth. Add the remaining icing sugar and one tablespoon of the milk and beat the mixture until creamy and smooth. Beat in more milk if necessary to loosen the icing.

7 Swirl the topping onto the cupcakes and top with sweets of your choice.

TOP TIP!
Use a fork to eat some of the creamier cupcakes! You don't want to make a mess!

BIRTHDAY CUPCAKES

Extra equipment:
- candles

Ingredients:
- 125 g (4 ½ oz) self-raising flour
- 125 g (4 ½ oz) butter, softened
- 125 g (4 ½ oz) caster sugar
- 2 large eggs
- 2–3 tablespoons milk

For the topping:
- a few drops of vanilla essence
- whipped cream
- sugar sprinkles
- candles, to decorate

1 Preheat the oven to 180°C / 350°F / gas mark 4.

2 Sift the flour into a bowl, followed by the butter. Use the tips of your fingers to rub the butter and flour together until the mixture becomes crumbly. Alternatively, ask an adult to use an electric whisk.

3 Add the sugar and mix it in, then stir in the eggs.

4 Finally, add the milk to make the mixture creamy.

5 Put spoonfuls of the mixture into the bun cases. Bake the cupcakes for 10–15 minutes, until they are golden brown, then leave them to cool on a wire rack.

6 For the topping, add the vanilla essence to the whipped cream an then swirl over each of the cupcakes.

7 Then, top each with sugar sprinkle and a candle.

TOP TIP!
Try colour coordinating your sugar sprinkles with your candles and cases!

CHEEKY CHERRY CUPCAKES

Equipment:
...der
...g bag

Ingredients:
...g (4 ½ oz) butter, softened
...g (4 oz) dark chocolate,
...en into pieces
...g (10 ½ oz) morello
...ry jam
...g (5 oz) caster sugar
...rge eggs, beaten
...g (5 oz) self-raising flour

...e topping:
...g (4 oz) cherries, chopped
...g (5 oz) butter, softened
...w drops of vanilla essence
...easpoons cherry juice
...g (10 oz) icing sugar
...ops red food colouring
...fresh or glacé cherries,
...decorate

1 Preheat the oven to 180°C / 350°F / gas mark 4.

2 Put the butter in a pan and ask an adult to melt it on a medium heat. When nearly melted, stir in the chocolate. Take off the heat and stir until the mixture is smooth and melted.

3 Now, add the cherry jam, sugar, and eggs. Stir well to combine.

4 Next, sift in the self-raising flour, and mix well.

5 Put spoonfuls of the mixture into the bun cases. Bake the cupcakes for 10–15 minutes, then leave them to cool on a wire rack.

6 For the topping, place the chopped cherries in a blender and ask an adult to process until smooth. Once smooth, add to a bowl, along with the butter, vanilla essence and juice. Then, sift in the icing sugar, add the red food colouring and mix well.

7 Place the topping into a piping bag and pipe onto each cupcake. Finish with a fresh or glacé cherry.

TOP TIP!
You can use fresh or glacé cherries for this cheeky recipe!

LEMON MERINGUE CUPCAKES

TOP TIP! If you have any left over meringue crumble it in a bowl and top with fresh berries and cream!

MAKES 12

Extra equipment:
- blender
- piping bag

Ingredients:
- 100 g (4 oz) caster sugar
- 100 g (4 oz) butter, softened
- 2 eggs
- zest 2 lemons
- 2–3 tablespoons lemon juice
- 100 g (4 oz) self-raising flour
- 4 tablespoons lemon curd

For the topping:
- 140 g (5 oz) butter, softened
- 280 g (10 oz) icing sugar
- 1–2 tablespoons lemon juice
- a few drops of yellow food colouring
- 1 shop-bought meringue
- sugar sprinkles

1 Preheat the oven to 180°C / 350°F / gas mark 4.

2 Put the sugar and butter in a bowl and beat well together. Add the eggs, one by one, mixing in well each time.

3 Stir in the zest and a squeeze of lemon juice, then fold in the flour. If the mixture is a bit stiff, add more lemon juice.

4 Put spoonfuls of the mixture into the bun cases, filling them halfway. Add 1 teaspoon of lemon curd and then top with the remaining mixture. Bake the cupcakes for 10–15 minutes, until they are golden brown, then leave them to cool on a wire rack.

5 For the topping, place the butter in large bowl and add half of the icing sugar. Beat until smooth.

6 Add the remaining icing sugar, one tablespoon of the lemon juice, and few drops of yellow food colouring. Beat the mixture until creamy and smooth. Beat in more lemon juice if necessary to loosen the icing.

7 Then, break up the meringue into tiny pieces. Add to the topping mixture and mix in thoroughly.

8 Place in a piping bag and pipe on top of each cupcake. Finish with sugar sprinkles.

ARAMEL CUPCAKES

ents:

g (4 oz) dark chocolate

g (5 oz) butter

g (5 oz) brown sugar

g (3 oz) golden syrup

ml (5 fl.oz) milk

g (4 ½ oz) plain flour

g (2 oz) self-raising flour

gg, lightly beaten

e topping:

g (1 oz) butter, softened

g (2 oz) soft brown sugar

ablespoons single cream

g (4 oz) icing sugar

colate, to decorate

ge, to decorate

1 Preheat the oven to 180°C / 350°F / gas mark 4.

2 Place the chocolate, butter, brown sugar, syrup and milk in a small saucepan. Ask an adult to stir over a low heat until melted and smooth. Leave to cool for about 15 minutes.

3 Sift the plain flour and self-raising flour into a bowl.

4 Then add the flour into the caramel mixture. Next, stir in the egg. Mix until combined.

5 Use a teaspoon to transfer equal amounts of the mixture into the bun cases. Bake the cupcakes for about 20 minutes. Leave them to cool on a wire rack.

6 For the topping, ask an adult to melt the butter and sugar in a saucepan. Bring to the boil, add the cream and simmer for 5 minutes. Remove from the heat and sift in the icing sugar. Beat until smooth.

7 Swirl over the cupcakes and top with smaller pieces of chocolate and fudge.

TOP TIP!
Experiment with the decorations! Why not try sugar sprinkles or chopped chocolate bars for the topping?

CHOCOLATE FUDGE CUPCAKES

Ingredients:
- 50 g (2 oz) caster sugar
- 50 g (2 oz) soft brown sugar
- 100 g (4 oz) butter, softened
- 2 eggs
- 2 tablespoons sweetened condensed milk
- 125 g (4 ½ oz) self-raising flour
- 1 teaspoon baking powder
- 25 g (1 oz) unsweetened cocoa powder

For the topping:
- 150 g (5 oz) butter
- 150 g (5 oz) sifted icing sugar
- 4 tablespoons cocoa powder
- 3 tablespoons milk
- sugar sprinkles, to decorate

1 Preheat the oven to 180°C / 350°F / gas mark 4.

2 Place both sugars and the butter into a bowl and beat together until smooth.

3 Then, add the eggs, one at a time, and mix well.

4 Add the condensed milk and then sift in the flour, baking powder and cocoa powder, making sure they are well mixed.

5 Put spoonfuls of the mixture into the bun cases. Bake the cupcakes for 20–25 minutes, then leave them to cool on a wire rack.

6 For the topping, place the butter in a large bowl and add half of the icing sugar. Beat until smooth.

7 Add the remaining icing sugar, cocoa powder and one tablespoon of the milk and beat the mixture until creamy and smooth. Beat in more milk if necessary to loosen the icing.

8 Swirl the topping onto each of the cupcakes and finish with sugar sprinkles.

TOP TIP! Make this cupcake even more gooey by adding chopped pieces of fudge to the topping!

PRICOT CUPCAKES

equipment:

ng bag

ents:

g (4 oz) self-raising flour

g (4 ½ oz) butter,
ened

g (4 ½ oz) caster sugar

rge eggs

g (4 oz) ready-to-eat
cots, chopped

tablespoons milk

e topping:

g (5 oz) butter, softened

g (10 oz) icing sugar

ablespoon apricot jam

rop orange food colouring

1 Preheat the oven to 180°C / 350°F / gas mark 4.

2 Sift the flour into a bowl, followed by the butter. Use the tips of your fingers to rub the butter and flour together until the mixture becomes crumbly. Alternatively, ask an adult to use an electric whisk.

3 Add the sugar and mix it in, then stir in the eggs.

4 Finally, add the chopped apricots and milk to make the mixture creamy.

5 Put spoonfuls of the mixture into the bun cases. Bake the cupcakes for 10–15 minutes, until they are golden brown, then leave them to cool on a wire rack.

6 For the topping, place the butter in a large bowl and add half of the icing sugar. Beat until smooth.

7 Add the remaining icing sugar, and one tablespoon of apricot jam and the food colouring and beat the mixture until creamy and smooth. Beat in some milk if necessary to loosen the icing.

8 Place into a piping bag and pipe the topping onto the cupcakes.

TOP TIP!
You can use either dried or fresh apricots depending on availability.

INDEX OF RECIPES

Heavenly Cupcakes

Packed with over 25 cupcake recipes!

From luscious lavender and cheeky cherry to beautiful banoffee and melt-in-the-mouth marshmallow, simply follow the step-by-step instructions to create a range of delightful cupcakes that are perfect for children and adults to make together!

Top THAT™

Licensed exclusively to Top That Publishing Ltd
Tide Mill Way, Woodbridge, Suffolk, IP12 1AP, UK
www.topthatpublishing.com
Copyright © 2014 Tide Mill Media.
All rights reserved
0 2 4 6 8 9 7 5 3 1
Printed and bound in China

ADULT SUPERVISION IS REQUIRED
FOR ALL RECIPES IN THIS BOOK

RRP £6.99
ISBN 978-1-78445-276-6

9 781784 452766

IT-CFG-32-1409-16

KQ-064-757

Jungle war

The Africans developed a form of fighting called 'jungle war' to protect themselves and their settlements. Ex-slaves would go into the plantations and teach this style of fighting to those who were still captive. To avoid suspicion, they introduced music and acrobatic elements to the fighting, leading the slave masters to believe that they were dancing. This fighting to music became known as capoeira.

Capoeira today

When Brazil outlawed slavery in 1850, many former slaves continued to dance. In the harsh conditions on the Brazilian streets, capoeira became associated with gangs and street fights, and it was banned in 1892. The ban was lifted in 1918, and Brazil's first capoeira school opened in 1932. Today, as the sport continues to grow, there are capoeira schools in more than 130 countries around the world.

PULLING RANK

Like other martial arts, capoeira has a ranking system. Capoeiristas work hard over many years to achieve the next grade – and the respect of their fellow capoeiristas.

The student

Once a person starts playing capoeira, he or she is called an *aluno* or student. The student has a baptism (*batizado*) where they are given their own ranking cord or belt (*a cordão*) to wear around their waist. Sometimes, the student is given a nickname (*apelido*). Usually, the nickname refers to some aspect of a player's character or appearance.

The graduate

When a student is good enough to teach others, he or she becomes a graduate and is called an *aluno graduado*. While the graduate can teach others how to play, they cannot be the main teacher or have their own capoeira school.

The teacher

Once a capoeirista is good enough to be an assistant instructor, he or she is called an *aluno formado*. After several years of training under their capoeira master (*mestre*), an *aluno formado* can become a teacher and then they may run their own capoeira school.

Master of the sport

Mestre is the highest rank any capoeirista can achieve. A *mestre* is a teacher who has been given the title of master by others. Usually, the *mestre* has trained for 15 to 20 years. Mestre Bimba was one of the most well-known masters of capoeira. He dedicated himself to capoeira and worked tirelessly when the sport was banned, to make it legal again (see page 9).

DANCE OR FIGHT?

People who play capoeira believe this fusion of dance and martial arts is a great way to keep the body and mind healthy. They say:

1. The acrobatic moves work every muscle in the body. Players develop agility, strength and stamina.
2. The sport is a workout for the brain, too! You need to outsmart your opponent by being decisive and aware of his or her next move.
3. Capoeira is sociable. Players train in groups and every game is played inside a circle of people.
4. Capoeira builds self-esteem and good self-defence techniques.
5. Lessons are open to everyone, regardless of age or physical ability. Beginners are encouraged to develop at their own pace.
6. Players do not need expensive gear. Beginners start in tracksuit pants, a T-shirt and bare feet.
7. The rules of capoeira can help people to become more disciplined in their everyday lives.

However, some people think that capoeira is a dangerous martial art based on violent fighting moves. They say:

1. Doing acrobatics on a hard floor is dangerous because people can get thrown, kicked or knocked down. There is a high risk of injury.
2. It can take several years to train as an instructor. As the sport becomes more popular, some unqualified teachers may set up classes and put students at risk of injuries.
3. Capoeira classes can appear to be closed to 'outsiders' and joining in can be difficult.
4. The capoeira culture draws people in and can take over their lives much more than other types of martial art.
5. Players can start to feel aggressive and real fights have been known to break out inside the *roda*.

AGAINST

Right or wrong?

Like all martial arts, capoeira is a great way to exercise and learn new skills. It allows players to enjoy the competition and energy of combat without any physical contact. Capoeira is safe as long as it is carried out with proper guidance and training.

THE SWING

The swing (*ginga*) is the basis for all capoeira moves. Get this basic move right and it is game on!

You will need:

- **floor space** • **bare feet**
- **loose, comfortable clothes**

1

Step to the right, swing your left leg behind you, putting some weight onto it. At the same time, sweep your left arm round in front of you.

2

Bring your left leg forwards so that you are standing with your legs apart, knees bent.

3

Move your weight over to your left and swing your right leg behind you. Sweep your right arm in front of you.

Type 'basic steps *ginga*' into www.youtube.com to master this basic move!

4

Bring your right leg back so that you are in the same standing position as you were in step 2.

Got it?

Ginga means 'to swing' and if it is done correctly, you should move from side to side with a swaying motion. The *ginga* is used in preparation for other more complicated moves.

5

Shift your weight to your right leg and swing your left leg behind you again. Repeat the steps.

FIGHTING TALK

Know your *ginga* from your *jogo* with our ultimate guide to capoeira lingo!

agogô
an African musical instrument with two hollow wooden cones that are hit to create sound

aluno
a student of capoeira

aluno formado
a capoeirista who is qualified to teach

aluno graduado
a capoeirista who is good enough to show others how to play but not qualified to have their own school or assist a teacher

atabaque
a large wooden drum

aú (cartwheel)
a capoeira move very similar to a cartwheel

bateria
the group of musical instruments played at a *jogo*. It may include *pandeiros*, *reco-recos* and *agogôs*

berimbau
a musical instrument that looks like a large bow with a hollowed out gourd attached to the bottom

boca de calça (hems of the pants)
a capoeira takedown that is executed by grabbing and pulling the opponent's trouser legs or ankles

canivete (jack knife)
a capoeira move used to attack or dodge opponents

capoeirista
someone who plays capoeira

ginga (swing)
the basic move of capoeira

jogo
a game of capoeira

macaquinho (little monkey)
an acrobatic escape move that means 'little monkey' in Portuguese

martelo (hammer)
a lightning-fast kick used in capoeira

meia lua de frente (half moon)
a powerful kick in which the player makes a crescent (half moon) shape when they swing the leg

mestre
the highest rank a capoeirista can have

pandeiro
a type of tambourine played as part of the *bateria*

reco-reco
a musical instrument that is usually made from a section of bamboo with grooves cut into the side. It is played by rubbing a stick over the grooves

roda
a circle of capoeira players in which *jogos* are played

takedown
a move in which a player forces his opponent to the floor

pandeiro

GLOSSARY

adrenalin
a hormone found in the human body that causes the heart to beat faster

captive
to be held against your will

choreograph
to devise a routine, usually in dancing

enchant
to fascinate and captivate

evade
to get around or avoid

fusion
a mixture of two or more different things

martial art
a combat-based sport which often teaches self-discipline and defence rather than aggression

outmanoeuvre
move more effectively than someone else

plantations
large farms where crops were grown and harvested by slaves

self-esteem
confidence in and respect for yourself

settlement
a place where a group of people live

spar
an unaggressive fight in which attack and defence moves are practised

stamina
the ability to do something for a long time

17

MARK 'FERRADURA' OBSTFELD

Radar talks to Mark 'Ferradura' Obstfeld, talented capoeirista, at London's Muzenza school. Find out why he loves this 'beautiful and dangerous' sport...

How did you get into capoeira?

My friend was taught capoeira for his work as an acrobat and stuntman. One day he showed me some mind-blowing moves. I was so impressed that when I saw a poster advertising capoeira classes, I jumped at the chance.

Have you had any injuries?

I haven't been badly injured, but accidents can happen if you don't concentrate while your opponent is kicking. The acrobatics are also risky. It's important to train hard and wait until you're ready to take on difficult moves. A good teacher helps you every step of the way.

How has capoeira changed your life?

Capoeira has opened up my world and given me a massive confidence boost. I have met some of my best friends at Muzenza and I love training with them. We learn from each other but there's always that competitive edge, too – which keeps things interesting!

Gym workout or capoeira?

Capoeira! I've never been in better shape. My body is toned, I'm flexible and have I stacks of stamina. I could have gone to a gym, but it's great training with others. And if I'm ever in trouble, I know how to defend myself!

What does your capoeira name mean?

All capoeira names have some sort of meaning – mine means 'horseshoe'. Not because I'm lucky... but because the remains of the hair I once had now forms a horseshoe shape around the back of my head!

Ferradura (Mark, left) spars with a fellow Muzenza capoeirista.

What is the best way to start capoeira?

Find a school near you and give it a try! Don't be put off if you see other people speaking to each other in Portuguese and doing amazing moves. Remember, they were beginners once, too!

How young can you start?

My first *mestre* was six when he started capoeira and I've seen kids of three or four trying it. Anyone who can walk steadily can have a go at capoeira!

19

THE HEAT

Beats from the *berimbau* and *atabaque* fill the air. The rhythms pulse through your body and all thoughts fade from your mind as you focus on the contest. Your body feels powerful and free under your light clothes. Energised by the anticipation in the air, which is crackling like electricity, you move into the *roda*, clapping and singing with the group. Let the *jogo* begin!

Lightning speed

A capoeirista cartwheels into the ring, inviting you to spar. You launch yourself into the centre, feeling a dizzying rush of air as you flip onto your hands. Then you swoop down into a swaying *ginga*, concentrating on your next move. Every muscle in your body is tense and ready to burst into action.

Type 'capoeira *roda*' into www.youtube.com to hear the beats and see the action!

Explosive energy

The beat of the music pulses through your body and a wave of adrenalin surges through your veins. All eyes are fixed on you and your opponent. You focus on her every move and your body reacts, driven by the energy of the music and the clapping crowd. She comes at you with a wild leg sweep but you cartwheel out of danger. You roll away to escape a spinning kick and flip into a handstand. You're on top form and she can't get close.

Eye to eye

As the *jogo* ends you look your partner in the eye. You were graceful and powerful. She backs out of the *roda* with a nod of respect. You feel so alive and ready to take on anything. When you have played the game well there is no feeling that touches it.

LIGHTS, CAMERA, CAPOEIRA!

A new martial arts craze is sweeping the world. Capoeira blends high-energy fighting skills with mesmerising dance moves. It is springing up everywhere from Hollywood films to television adverts. What makes it so popular?

Arresting moves

The striking acrobatic moves of capoeira make people stop and stare. In 2002, a short film clip used by the BBC as a programme link introduced capoeira to UK viewers. Since then, the sport has featured in adverts for everything from soft drinks to mobile phones.

Hollywood style

Capoeiristas can choreograph impressive fight scenes, without injuries or special effects – no wonder they're in demand with filmmakers! Capoeira's elegant flips and kicks made it the obvious choice for Halle Berry's role in *Catwoman* (2004). The actress trained with a top *mestre* before shooting her fight scenes.

Capoeria has also worked its magic in *Harry Potter and the Goblet of Fire* (2005). Its high-energy moves showcased the amazing strength and agility of the Durmstrang pupils. But in the movies, the opponent is not always another person! A thief in *Ocean's Twelve* (2004), for example, used capoeira moves to outmanoeuvre a laser security system.

Capoeira fever!

Today the public have gone capoeira crazy. The Afro-Brazilian sport is spicing up parties, concerts and awards shows all over the world. Capoeira moves are music video scene-stealers (take a look at The Black Eyed Peas *Mas Que Nada* music video), and capoeirista clips get millions of hits online. So get out there and find a class to see what the fuss is all about!

In its native Brazil, many very young children practise capoeira.

'Capoeira is probably the hardest thing on the planet to learn to do,' says Halle Berry. 'And I had to learn how to do everything in high heels!'

23

THE HALF MOON

Start with a basic
swing move
(see page 14).

1

This 'half moon kick' (*meia lua de frente*) gets its name from the half circle drawn by the kicking leg.

You will need:

- floor space • bare feet
- loose, comfortable clothes

Type '*meia lua de frente – capoeira*' into www.youtube.com to see how the half moon kick works.

2

Step out of the swing on your left foot, lifting your right leg to the side and up as you do so.

24

3

Continue to swing your leg around in a half moon shape in front of your body. Try to lift your leg up high but take care not to fall over!

5

Step back on your right leg, crouching slightly as you land your foot and get ready for your next move.

4

Bring your leg across your body and down to the left. Twist your body to keep balance.

Got it?

Your right leg should have made a semi-circle shape in front of your body. You should have kept your body steady and used your arms for balance by moving them in the opposite direction to the swing of your leg.

THE MOVES

hems of the pants

jack knife

cartwheel

little monkey

hammer

Players try to outsmart their opponent with leg sweeps, takedowns and kicks. At the same time they defend themselves with dynamic acrobatics, rolls and ducks. Here are some of the best basic moves.

jack knife (*canivete*)

This is a clever move used for attack or defence. Players begin in the same way as a cartwheel to fool the opponent into moving close so the player can deliver an unexpected 'kick' or 'strike'.

hems of the pants (*boca de calça*)

This amazing takedown is performed by pulling the opponent's legs from underneath them as their other leg passes above the player's head.

cartwheel (*aú*)

This defensive move is similar to a cartwheel. It is used by a player to spin away from an attacking opponent.

little monkey (*macaquinho*)

This nifty ground move allows the player to move quickly out of danger. Players keep the upper body facing forwards as they roll the legs backwards from a crouching position.

hammer (*martelo*)

In this fast-moving strike, the player kicks one foot at the opponent – aiming for the head – while keeping the other foot on the ground. The shin or instep of the foot can be used to land this kick.

Type 'capoeira *macaquinho*' into www.youtube.com to see it in use.

CAPOEIRA STYLE

Capoeira is fast and free-flowing, so loose, comfortable clothes are important. Beginners can start in simple tracksuit pants and T-shirt.

Classic whites

Many capoeiristas wear white. This tradition was formalised by Mestre Bimba, who set up the world's first official capoeira school in Bahia, Brazil. Students wore white uniforms to show that capoeira was about respect and discipline, and not about gangs and fighting.

Kitted out

Most capoeira groups have their own uniform – often loose, stretchy white trousers (*abadas*) and a shirt. T-shirts are fitted so that they do not fall over a player's head during handstands.

Loose, stretchy trousers allow players to perform acrobatic moves.

Feet first

Players go barefoot or wear lightweight, non-slip shoes. Inexperienced capoeiristas may also wear non-slip gloves to help with handstands and cartwheels.

Members of the *roda* play music with the *berimbaus* and *pandeiros* of the *bateria*.

Accessories

As capoeiristas learn more about the roots of their sport, many wear strings of Brazilian beads (*padua*) that jangle as they play. Some capoeiristas carry their own *berimbau*, the stringed instrument played during the dance.

berimbau

Winning belts

Capoeiristas wear a rope (*cordão*) around their waists like a belt. As in other martial arts, capoeiristas work towards coloured belts that show their rank or level. The first is called the baptism (*batizado*) belt. It can take a year to build the skill, discipline, musical ability and knowledge of the game needed to earn each new *cordão*.

THE HAMMER

Start with a basic swing move (see page 14). From this move, step forward on your left foot.

1

2

The word *martelo* means 'hammer' indicating that this kick is fast and furious!

You will need:

- floor space • bare feet
- loose, comfortable clothes

Move your weight onto your left foot and as you do so, lift your right leg, with your knee bent.

3

Quickly extend your leg and kick it up to head height. Put your arm up to protect your face (if you were using this move while sparring you would be prepared for another's 'attacks').

4

Bring your leg back down. Use your arms to steady yourself, and then continue the swing.

Type 'capoeira *martelo*' into www.youtube.com to see how the hammer kick works.

Got it?

You should have swung the leg and delivered your kick with maximum power. To defend yourself from a counter-attack after a hammer, you should hold your arms in front of your face.

31

GET THE BRAZILIAN BUG!

People to talk to

If you want a high-energy workout for your body and brain, capoeira is for you. And your timing couldn't be better – groups and schools are opening up all over the country! Search online to find a class near you.

The Muzenza school

If you want to practise capoeira with Radar's Mark Obstfeld, check out Instructor Bombril's Muzenza school at: **www.capoeiracademyuk.com**

Sign up to the huge online capoeira community and check out videos, music and photos of the sport at: **www.capoeira.com**

DVDs, Reads & Apps

Read, watch and learn more about this energy-charged dance sport.

Capoeira: Game! Dance! Martial Art! George Ancona (Lee & Low, Children's Edition 2007)

100% Capoeira: 3 Films (2005)

Check out the *Capoeira* app at: **www.itunes.com**

INDEX